HOW THINGS WORK

How does a torch work?

A torch is powered by batteries.

A torch has a bulb and batteries. When a torch is switched on, an electric current comes from the batteries and

passes into the bulb. This causes the bulb to light up. The current to the bulb is stopped by switching the torch off again.

How does a bicycle dynamo work?

Inside a bicycle dynamo, are magnets around a bobbin with a copper thread wound round it. When the drivewheel of the dynamo rubs against the turning wheel of a bicycle, the bobbin turns and a magnetic field is created.
This causes an electric current to light up the bulb in the lamp.

The dynamo lights a bicycle lamp.

3

How do mirrors work?

A mirror is usually made of glass with a thin layer of silver or aluminium on the back. This means that rays of light reflect off the glass

instead of passing through it. When you look in a mirror, you see a mirror-image. A mirror-image makes your right side become your left and vice versa. Hold up your left hand in front of a mirror. Which hand has the mirror-image lifted?

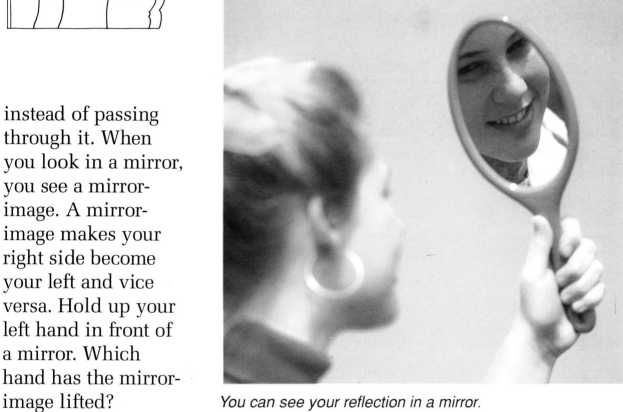

You can see your reflection in a mirror.

Why do we use egg-timers?

An egg-timer contains fine sand which pours through a narrow hole between the top and bottom parts. The sand always takes the same time to do this, so the timer can be used to measure time.

How does a thermostat work?

When objects are heated, they expand (get bigger) and when they cool down, they contract (get smaller). A thermostat usually contains a strip of iron and a strip of copper, stuck together. These metals expand and contract at different temperatures.

A radiator thermostat controls temperature.

A radiator thermostat contains a liquid which expands when it is heated. When the liquid expands, it pushes against a plug which stops hot water from entering the radiator. When the liquid cools and contracts, the plug allows water to pass through again.

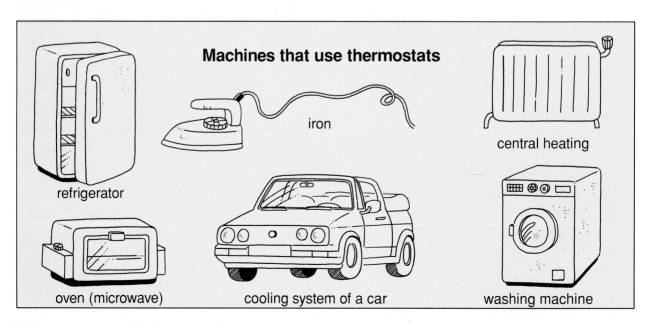

Machines that use thermostats

refrigerator

iron

central heating

oven (microwave)

cooling system of a car

washing machine

How does a filter coffee machine work?

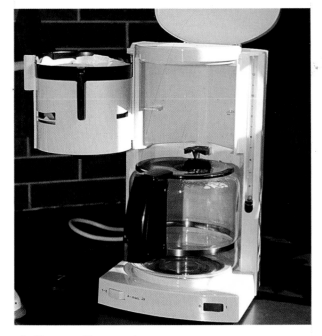

A filter coffee maker.

Water is poured into the back of the machine and heated. The hot water produces steam which creates enough pressure to force the water up a tube and through a filter containing ground coffee. The hot water is flavoured with the coffee as it drips into a container below.

How do trains avoid colliding?

Many trains travel on the rail tracks at the same time, but they do not collide. This is because they run to timetables and a points system is used.

When a train passes over a point in the track it sends a signal to a computer. If there is another train coming on the same track, the computer diverts it on to a different one.

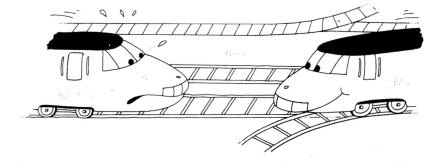

There are many tracks and points at a railway station.

How are tunnels built?

The shield protects workers from falling rocks.

Before engineers dig a tunnel, they study the soil and rock. Hard rock is broken by explosives and then bulldozers take away most of the soil and stones. Next, the tunnel shield is put into action. This shield is an enormous steel tube, the size of the intended tunnel. The shield is forced into the earth and the workmen are protected by it as they dig out the soil and rocks.

What is an electronic eye?

An electronic eye beams out a ray of light which is reflected by a mirror. When the ray of light is broken, the machine starts up or stops. Electronic eyes may be used to start or stop an escalator.

An electronic eye on an escalator.

How does a ballpoint pen work?

At the tip of a ballpoint pen, is a tiny metal ball. When you write, the ball turns round and ink in the pen is smeared over it.

ball

Why do boomerangs come back?

Boomerangs are specially shaped.

A boomerang is a piece of curved wood. It has to be thrown with a special twisting action that makes it rotate as it flies through the air. Once the force from the throw has lessened, the boomerang stops its flight forward. Its weight and the rotating movement cause it to turn and fly back.

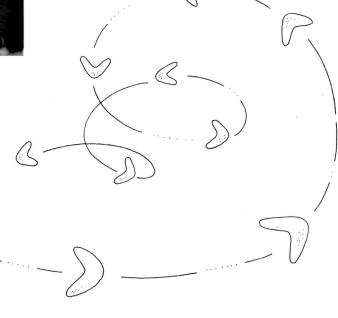

A quartz watch keeps good time.

How does a quartz watch work?

Inside a quartz watch is a tiny quartz crystal. The electric current from a battery makes the quartz crystal vibrate.
The regular vibrations set off a tiny motor which turns the hands of the watch.
A quartz watch does not need to be wound up.

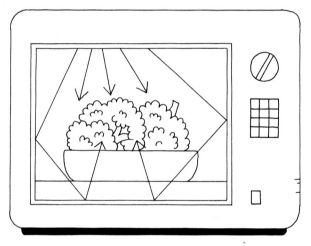

How does a micro-wave oven work?

A microwave oven uses microwaves to heat food. All food contains water, and the oven uses rays of electromagnetic

radiation to heat the water molecules in food. A fan or turntable allows the microwaves to penetrate food from all angles so that it is heated evenly.
Many microwaves have grills which give food a browned, crisp look as if it has come out of an oven.

A microwave oven cooks food quickly.

The history of the telephone

How do telephones work?

A telephone with buttons instead of a dial.

At one end of the handpiece of a telephone is a transmitter, at the other is a receiver. If you speak into the transmitter, the microphone inside it transforms the sound waves into electric impulses. These are transmitted through the telephone cable to the other person's receiver.

The receiver turns the impulses into sounds which are almost identical to the caller's voice.

How does an organ work?

An organ works like a flute. Each note is blown from a different pipe. Air used to be pumped by hand into the pipes using bellows, but nowadays it is pumped by an electronic device.

How are electronic timers used to time races?

In many sports, it is speed that counts and if competitors finish a race together, it is difficult to tell who was the fastest. This is why

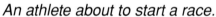

An athlete about to start a race.

electronic timers are used to time competitors to 100th of a second. The timekeeping equipment is set off when the race starts by the firing of the starter's pistol.

When an athlete crosses the finishing line, a beam of light is broken. When the light is broken, the timer records the exact time and this is printed out.

How does a hovercraft stay above water?

A hovercraft can travel faster than a boat.

A hovercraft forces out air underneath its front end. Large, rounded 'skirts' trap the air and the hovercraft is lifted clear of the water. This enables it to move swiftly along. Propellers on top and at the back of the craft propel it along and steer its direction.

How do bulbs work?

Inside a bulb is a thin piece of curved wire called a filament. The filament is made of a brittle metal with a high melting point called tungsten. When a light is turned on, an electric current passes across the filament which reaches a temperature of 2500°C! The heat makes the filament glow.

An electric light bulb.

Can a letter be sent using telephone lines?

Yes, by using a fax machine. A number is dialled on a fax machine. When it is answered, the letter passes through the machine and the writing is transformed into electric impulses. These are turned back into writing on special paper at the other end.

A fax machine transmits letters down telephone lines.

How do traffic lights work?

Traffic and pedestrian lights.

The lights of most traffic lights change according to a precise timing system which never varies. However, some modern lights calculate the number of vehicles that are waiting and others give priority to a lane of traffic with buses. Some buses have a transmitter whose signals are picked up by a machine inside the lights.

13

How do submarines stay under water?

A submarine contains large tanks of air.
When these tanks are full of air, the submarine floats.
When the submarine has to dive, the tanks are filled with water and it sinks.
When the submarine has to return to the surface, the water is pumped out and the tanks are filled with air again.
This new supply comes from compressed air. This is air that is pressed into a smaller space than it would usually take up.

A submarine in a harbour.

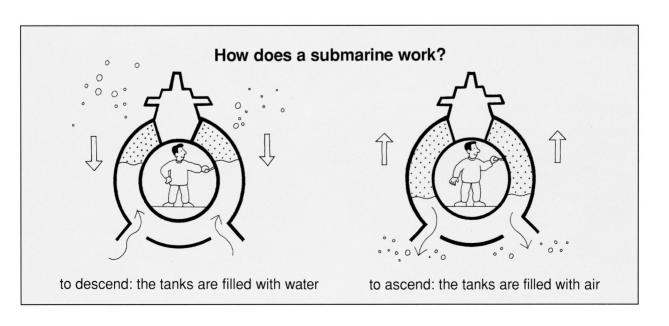

How does a submarine work?

to descend: the tanks are filled with water   to ascend: the tanks are filled with air

How are igloos made?

An igloo is built of blocks of ice. These blocks are larger at the base than at the top. They are arranged in a dome shape. At the front is an opening for air.

How does a compass work?

The needle of a compass is in fact a magnet. The ends of this magnet always point to north and south because they are attracted by the magnetic fields at the North and South Poles.

A compass tells you which direction is north.

You can use a magnet to make a compass. Rub one end of a magnet in the same direction against a needle about 50 times. Push the needle through a cork and float it in a bowl of water. One end of the needle will point to north. Check which end it is with a compass.

How is a cinema film made?

This film is being shot in the jungle.

A film is made from long strips of thousands of tiny negatives. Each negative is an undeveloped photograph. When the negatives are passed quickly in front of a light at a speed of about 24 images per second, the images seem to move.

How does a microphone work?

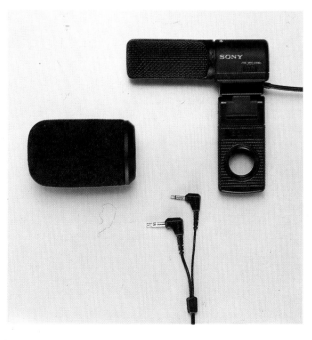

Inside a microphone is a metal disc that vibrates at the slightest sound. Vibrations pass to an amplifier as electric signals. The amplifier uses the signals to send sounds out of a loudspeaker.

A microphone picks up sound.

What is cable television?

Cable televisions do not need aerials.

Images on national television are broadcast by TV stations. However, programmes on cable television are transmitted on an underground cable link and the television owners have to pay extra for this service.

Programmes may be transmitted from foreign countries by satellite. The satellite transmits the images to a master antenna installed at the cable network centre.

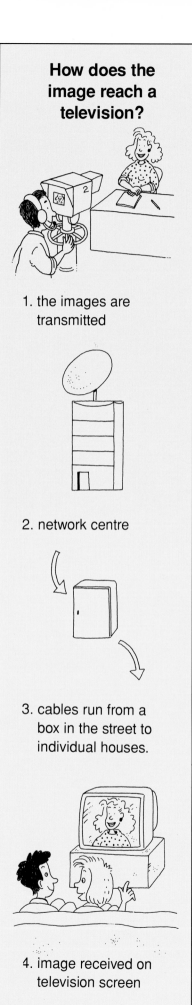

How does the image reach a television?

1. the images are transmitted

2. network centre

3. cables run from a box in the street to individual houses.

4. image received on television screen

How do helicopters fly?

Instead of wings, a helicopter has horizontal blades, called rotors, that whirl round and round very quickly. The bottom part of a rotor is flat while the top side is curved. When the rotors turn, an

A helicopter hovering in the sky.

area of low pressure is created above each one and this lifts the helicopter upwards. The rotors are slightly tilted to direct the helicopter in different directions.

How do answering machines work?

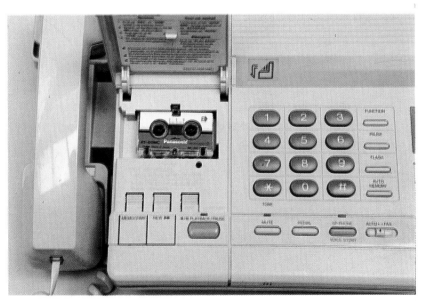

An answering machine records messages when you are out.

An answering machine is a combination of telephone and cassette recorder. When a telephone rings, a recorded message is played automatically. The caller speaks into the telephone and leaves a message which is recorded on a cassette.

How do sunbeds work?

If you stay in the Sun long enough, your skin turns brown. It does this because of the ultraviolet rays that come from the Sun. These rays cause your skin to produce more pigment which protects you from the Sun and makes you look brown. Ultraviolet rays can also be produced artificially by a special lamp. The lamp is often long enough to lie on, or under, while skin becomes tanned.

A sun-ray lamp can give you a tan indoors.

Why do some kettles whistle?

When water is heated, it turns into steam. Some kettles have a whistle on the spout and this makes a sharp, high noise when the steam from boiling water passes through it.

A whistle on the spout of a kettle.

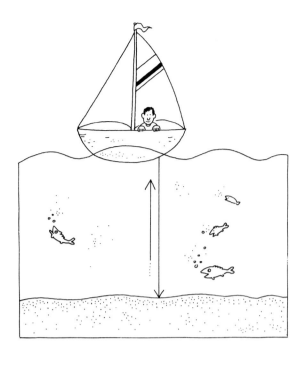

How is the depth of an ocean measured?

The depth of an ocean is measured by an ultrasonic sounder which bounces a high sound (higher than a human can hear) against the bottom of an ocean. The echo is recorded. The longer it takes for the echo to return, the deeper the ocean.

How does a mobile telephone work?

The number of a mobile telephone has a special code number in front of it. This code number connects a caller to a central system where a computer connects the call to a mobile telephone. This connection is made using local radio transmitters.
Some cars have mobile phones that do not have to be picked up. This means that the driver can answer the call and use both hands for driving.

Some cars are fitted with mobile phones.

What is Braille?

Braille is a special sort of writing for blind people. Each letter and number is represented by a combination of six raised dots of different thickness. The blind person reads the words by feeling the pattern of the points with his fingertips.

A special typewriter is used for writing Braille.

A Frenchman called Louis Braille, who was blind himself, invented this system of reading and writing.

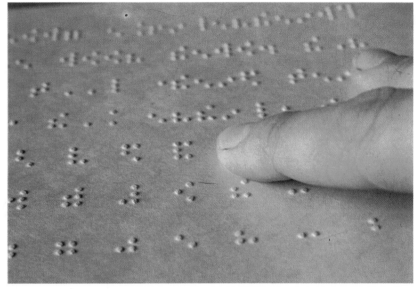

Blind people read Braille with their fingertips.

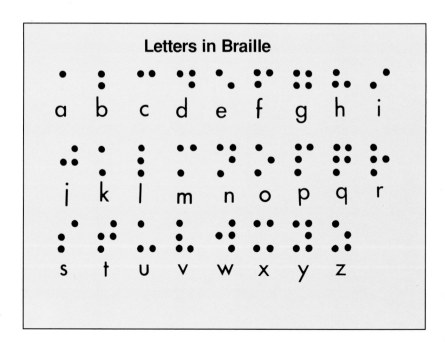

Numbers in Braille

1 2 3

4 5 6

7 8 9

0

Letters in Braille

a b c d e f g h i

j k l m n o p q r

s t u v w x y z

Why do cars have alarms?

A car alarm goes off if the doors or windows of a car are opened. Unless the person getting into the car has a key to turn the alarm off, it makes a loud noise. In this way, the alarm warns the owner if someone tries to steal the car. Some modern alarms can be operated by a remote control device.

A car alarm warns the owner of thieves.

Where does drinking water come from?

Most drinking water is pumped out of the ground.
Sometimes, drinking water is taken from reservoirs or lakes. In this case it is purified before it is pumped into the pipes that take it to houses and buildings.

Water is stored in a water tower.

How do nutcrackers work?

The best way to crack nuts is to use a nutcracker.

There are many types and designs of nutcrackers. The simplest and probably the most common is a nutcracker made of two bars of metal connected at one end by a hinge. A

nut is placed close to the hinge between the two bars. To crack the nut the two free ends of the bars are pushed together. The closer the nut is to the hinge, the easier it is to crack. This nutcracker is a type of lever.

Can clothes be cleaned without water?

Certain materials should not be washed in the normal way with soap and water. They must be dry cleaned.
They are placed in a drum with a special chemical which dissolves grease and gets rid of dirt.

Clothes can be cleaned without water.

How does a vacuum flask work?

Inside a flask is a bottle which has two glass walls. Between these walls is a vacuum. Heat cannot pass through a vacuum and so the contents stay hot.

How does a compact disc work?

Sound on a compact disc is recorded by a laser beam. The laser engraves sounds as codes on to a surface of a compact disc. The codes are put on to the disc as pits and plateaux (smooth, raised surfaces). The disc is coated with a reflective material which either scatters or reflects light. When the disc is played, a laser beam shines on to the coded surface. The machine recognises the codes and transforms them into sounds.

A compact disc player.

How is spaghetti made?

Spaghetti is made of pasta.
Pasta is made from flour and water (sometimes, eggs or spinach are added too). The pasta dough is fed into a machine and pushed

Spaghetti is made from pasta.

out through holes. The long, thin strands of spaghetti are dried. They must be boiled in water before they become soft and ready to eat.

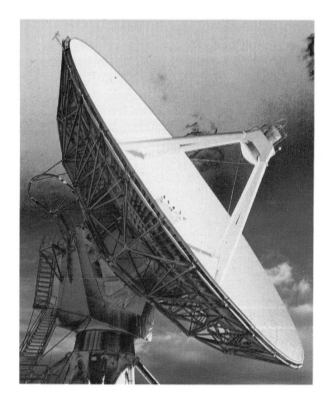

What is a satellite dish?

Images and sounds can be turned into waves. A satellite dish can transmit and receive these waves. The waves are transmitted to other countries by bouncing them off clouds or satellites. Satellite dishes are used for TV and radio transmissions.

A satellite dish.

How does a camera work?

Inside a camera is a roll of film coated with chemical substances. When the camera button is pressed, a shutter opens quickly letting light in. The light passes through a lens and is reflected onto a section of film. The chemicals on the film react and, when it is developed and printed on paper, each section becomes a photograph.

Taking photographs with a camera.

Objects with lenses

microscope

slide projector

glasses

magnifying glass

binoculars

telescope

Why does a fan cool air?

When the blades of a fan turn, they make the air move. Although the air temperature is the same, the moving air is refreshing and it cools us down.

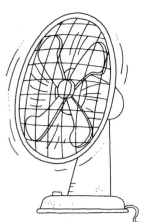

How do keys turn a lock?

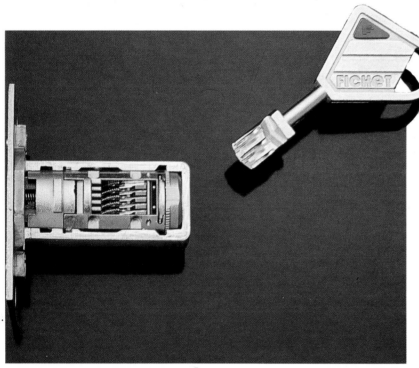

A special safety lock and key.

There are many sorts of locks and keys. Some locks are long, thin and fairly simple. Others are more complicated and have many ridges.

A lock usually has a set of pins inside a cylinder. These pins are raised by a key with a specially shaped edge. The edge of the key must be exactly the correct shape to raise the pins to a certain height or the lock will not turn. When the pins are raised, the cylinder turns and the lock is open.

What is a telephone camera?

A telephone camera transmits the images of a caller onto a screen. This enables people talking on the telephone to see each other.

A telephone camera may be used for security so that a person wanting to enter a building can be seen and recognised first.

A camera allows callers to see each other.

How does a doorbell work?

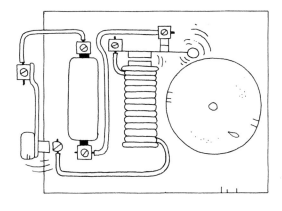

A visitor using a doorbell.

When the button on a doorbell is pressed, an electromagnet (an iron bar carrying an electric current) pushes a tiny hammer against a bell. But the hammer is connected to a spring which pulls it back. The hammer stops moving when the caller stops pressing the button.

Can a car have two engines?

Electric cars that use electricity do not give off poisonous fumes like cars that run on petrol or diesel. However, these cars cannot run for long without recharging their batteries. For this reason, a type of car has been invented that uses two engines, an electric one for short distances and a petrol one for longer distances.

Electric cars help to save the environment.

How do windmills make energy?

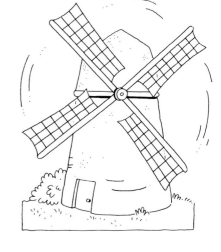

Wind makes the blades of a windmill spin round. At the centre of the blades is a cog (a toothed wheel) which, as it turns, produces

Wind is transformed into energy by windmills.

energy. Wind is an ideal source of energy. However, wind often changes direction and the blades have to be adjusted so that they are in the best position to use it. It is not easy to tell which direction the wind will blow from.

How do dams provide us with electricity?

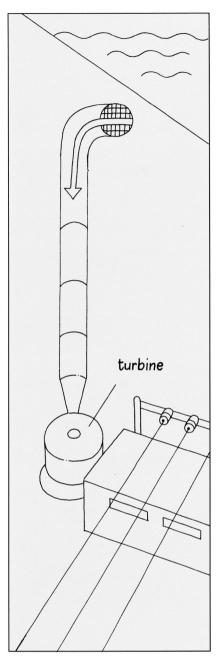

turbine

The wall of a dam holds water back. At the top of the dam, some water is let in which falls quickly down a pipe on to a turbine (a wheel) which it turns. As the turbine rotates, it drives a generator to produce electricity.

A hydro-electric dam provides electric power.

non-polluting sources of energy

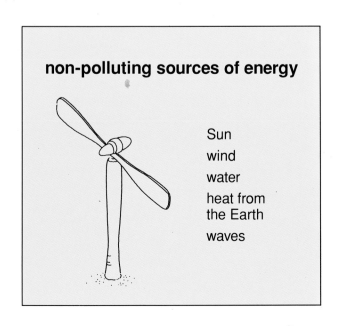

Sun
wind
water
heat from the Earth
waves

polluting sources of energy

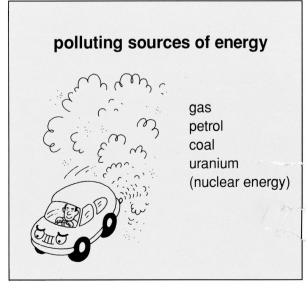

gas
petrol
coal
uranium
(nuclear energy)

How does a TV remote control work?

When you point a remote control at a television or video machine and press a button, it beams out an infra-red ray.

There are many types of remote control.

The ray sends a code which instructs the television to change channel or to adjust the volume. The television set has a receptor which decodes the signal and carries out the instructions. If there is an object between the remote control and the receptor, the infra-red ray will not be able to reach the television.

How does a dentist's drill work?

Inside a dental drill are two narrow tubes. Air is forced down one of the tubes and it is sucked up the other. The pressure of the air turns a small turbine which makes the burr on the end of the drill spin round at a high speed.

How does a barrier work?

A railway barrier.

A barrier is weighted at one end so the other end can be raised easily.

Barriers used to be raised by the action of an internal wheel and a crank. Nowadays, the wheel is powered by an engine.

How does an aeroplane stay in the air?

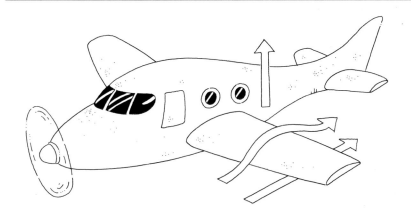

These aeroplanes fly high above the ground.

An aeroplane stays in the air because of the shape of its wings.

The wings curve outwards on the top side and they are flat on the lower side. This shape means that air passes faster over the wings than under them. This creates a lower pressure above each wing which results in an uplift.

The thrust that pushes an aeroplane through the air comes from propellers or jet engines.

Why are some foods vacuum packed?

Bacteria in the air can make food go bad. When foods, such as bacon and cheese, need to be kept for some time they are packed

Food is kept fresh when it is vacuum packed.

tightly in a clear plastic covering. The food is placed in a plastic bag and a machine sucks out all the air. Then the bag is tightly sealed so that no air can get in. When there is no air in the bag, it means that there is no bacteria and the food can stay fresh for longer.

How do zips work?

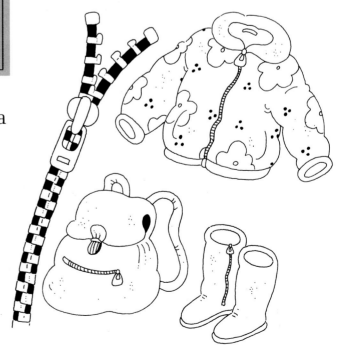

On each side of a zip fastener is a row of small metal, plastic or nylon teeth. When the zip fastener is pulled up, the teeth are brought together and they interlock. When the fastener is pulled down, the teeth are pushed apart.

Index

Sources of photographs

Agfa-Gevaert: 15 t; Alcatel Bell: 5 b, 9, 19, 24 b, 27 t; Bosch: 21 t; D'Ieteren: 28 t; Fishet F.: 26; Gety: 22 b; Hendrikx, I.: 2, 3, 4, 5 t, 6, 7, 8 t, 10, 11 t, 12 b, 13, 14, 17, 18 b, 20, 21 b, 22 b, 24 t, 25, 27 b, 28 b, 29, 31, 32; Philips: 11 b, 18 t, 23, 30; Philips Whirlpool: 8 b; Sony: 15 b, 16; Toshiba: 12 t.